D1298726

Chemical Reaction

The KidHaven Science Library

Chemical Reaction

by Roberta Baxter

KIDHAVEN PRESS
An imprint of Thomson Gale, a part of The Thomson Corporation

Detroit • New York • San Francisco • San Diego • New Haven, Conn. • Waterville, Maine • London • Munich

For more information, contact
KidHaven Press
27500 Drake Rd.
Farmington Hills, MI 48331-3535
Or you can visit our Internet site at http://www.gale.com

LIBRARY OF CONGRESS CATALOGING-IN-PUBLICATION DATA

Baxter, Roberta.
    Motion / by Roberta Baxter.
        p. cm. — (The KidHaven science library)
    Includes bibliographical references and index.
    ISBN 0-7377-2072-7 (hardback : alk. paper)

Printed in the United States of America

Contents

Chapter 1

What Are Chemical Reactions?

Chemical reactions happen around us all the time. Some occur naturally, as when the sun shines on a field of wheat. The sunshine reacts with chemicals in the wheat plant. The reaction makes food for the plant and so the plant grows bigger. Finally it produces wheat seed.

We can also *make* chemical reactions happen. After the wheat is harvested, the seed is ground into flour. The flour is mixed with other ingredients and put into an oven. Chemical reactions occur as the bread bakes. When the bread is done, we take it out of the oven and the chemical reactions stop. Chemical reactions turn the mixture of ingredients into bread.

As a person eats the bread, the chemical reaction known as **digestion** starts. Chemicals in a person's mouth mix with the bread. Chemical reactions turn the bread into energy for the body.

Chemical reactions occur when atoms meet and change into different substances. All matter is made up of **atoms**. Atoms are so small they cannot be seen in an ordinary microscope. About 250 million atoms would fit in one inch (2.5 cm).

Atoms are called the building blocks of nature because of the way they combine and break apart. When atoms combine, a **molecule** is formed. For

Chemical reactions help turn the dough this baker is mixing into loaves of bread.

example, a molecule of table salt is formed when an atom of sodium joins with an atom of chlorine.

A molecule can also break apart by chemical reaction. If the salt molecule breaks apart, an atom of sodium and an atom of chlorine will be left.

Physical Change or Chemical Change

With chemical changes, composition of the substances changes. This is different from physical changes. A physical change is one where the state of the substance changes but not its composition. For example, water has a molecule with three atoms, two of hydrogen and one of oxygen. Water that freezes has changed, but it is still water. It has not changed its composition. It still has two atoms of hydrogen and one of oxygen. Freezing is a physical change.

Physical changes can be easily reversed. If you warm up the ice, it melts back into water. And its composition, two hydrogen atoms and one oxygen atom, stays the same. This does not happen with chemical reactions. When a chemical reaction occurs, the beginning substances, called **reactants**, change into different substances called **products**. When sodium, a shiny bright metal, chemically reacts with chlorine, a poisonous green gas, the product is a white solid called sodium chloride (more commonly known as table salt). In this case a chemical change has occurred. The product is completely different from the two reactants.

A reaction always means there has been a chemical change and new products have been made. Chemical changes are only reversible through more chemical reactions. Table salt cannot be changed back into sodium metal and chlorine gas as easily as ice melting back into water. That change requires another chemical reaction.

The ice (inset) and snow on this frozen lake have the same composition as liquid water.

Why Do Reactions Happen?

What makes chemical reactions happen? The answer goes back to the smallest particle of matter, the atom.

Every atom contains a center called the nucleus. The nucleus has two types of particles, neutrons and protons. Orbiting the nucleus are **electrons**. The electrons are the parts of the atom that participate in chemical reactions.

Electrons orbit around the nucleus of an atom in this computer image.

Chemical reactions happen when atoms gain, lose, or share electrons. Electrons surround the nucleus of an atom in layers, called shells. For the most stable atom, the outer shell needs to be full of electrons. To get a full shell, atoms will take or give up electrons to other atoms or share electrons with another atom. A chemical reaction has taken place and a chemical **bond** has formed.

Electron Give and Take

Sodium has eleven electrons and ten of them are in shells close to the atom's nucleus. The single outside electron is in a shell by itself. To become more stable, sodium will easily give up that lone electron to have a full electron shell.

The extra electron goes to another atom that needs to add an electron to make a full shell. The outside shell of the chlorine atom needs six electrons to be full and it has only five. To add one electron, the chlorine atom takes an electron from sodium. This reaction forms a new compound, sodium chloride, or table salt. The atoms of sodium and chlorine have exchanged their electrons. Swapping electrons forms a bond between the atoms, making a molecule of table salt.

Sharing Electrons

Some atoms share electrons with each other rather than give them up or take them. The most common is carbon, which has four outer electrons to share. All living things have thousands of carbon compounds.

Carbon atoms bond easily with other carbon atoms. A gas called ethene contains two carbon atoms linked to each other. If thousands of ethene atoms react with each other, the plastic of a milk jug is formed. Plastic molecules have thousands of carbon atoms linked in long chains like beads on a necklace. The atoms react by sharing their electrons.

Reaction Rules

One characteristic of chemical reactions is that they are predictable. Chemical reactions happen the same way all the time if the conditions are the same. Because of this, factories can make huge batches of chemicals day after day and they will make the same product. So if a factory mixes certain chemicals and heats them for a certain amount of time on a Monday, the result is sodium bicarbonate or baking soda, a chemical used in baking. Then on Tuesday, the factory can mix those chemicals again and heat them the same way and still get sodium bicarbonate as the product of the reaction.

Another characteristic of reactions is that they happen at different speeds. When the iron of a nail combines with oxygen, it may take weeks or months for the nail to rust. But the reaction of oxygen and fuel in a rocket engine happens instantaneously and provides power to lift a spacecraft into orbit.

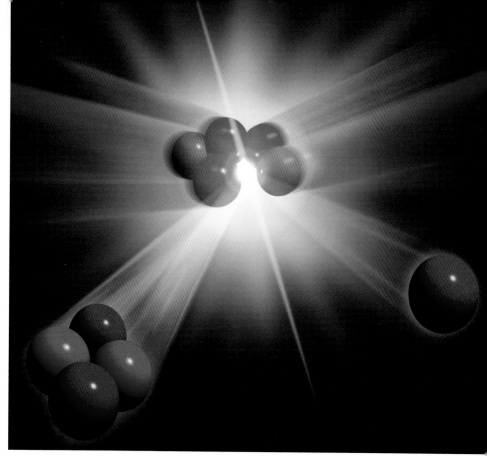

In this computer model, atoms bond together (center), forming a molecule (left) and releasing energy.

When atoms react, energy is released. Energy means the ability to do work. When atoms are alone, they contain energy. When they bond together into a molecule, that energy is released. The released energy might be heat, light, or the ability to move muscles. To break the bond, energy is absorbed. So molecules must get energy to break down into atoms. Usually that energy comes from the surroundings or from an energy source such as the sun.

What Are Chemical Reactions? 13

Combined Atoms

Similar to the atoms in a chemical reaction, when a set of wood blocks (left) is stacked together (right), the blocks form a new combination. Although the blocks have moved, no blocks have been added or lost.

Finally, atoms are not created or destroyed during chemical reactions. The atoms just get shuffled around. This can be understood by thinking of atoms as colored blocks. Two green blocks stuck together and a set with one orange and one blue represent reactants. After a reaction, the blocks have one set with green and orange blocks and one with green and blue blocks as the products. All the blocks are still there, but the combinations have changed, just as atoms do in chemical reactions.

Chapter 2

Kinds of Reactions

Chemical reactions can be grouped in different families of similar reactions. Knowing how one reaction happens can help chemists predict how another reaction in the same family will occur.

Acids and Bases React

Acids and bases form one family of reactions. These chemicals are commonly found around the house, as well as in factories and laboratories. Acids that are found in our homes include vinegar, citric acid in fruit such as oranges and lemons, and the very strong acid in a car battery. Familiar bases are baking soda, soaps, and the strong base in oven cleaners and drain cleaners.

Acids can be strong enough to eat away metal or mild enough to give a tangy taste to lemonade. The strength depends on the type of acid and how concentrated it is.

The opposite of acids are called bases. Bases can be strong enough to eat away human skin. Weaker basic compounds help us clean our bodies and our clothes. The strength of the base depends on its type and its concentration.

When an acid and a base are mixed together, they react and cancel each other out. After the reaction, the acid and base are gone. The products are water, salt, and sometimes other chemicals. The products in each reaction depend on what acid and base were mixed together.

The acid-base reaction can be seen in a common home experiment. In this experiment, vinegar, a weak acid, and baking soda, a weak base, are mixed together. The reaction produces water, salt, and carbon dioxide gas, which bubbles up out of the container.

Chemicals called indicators can help determine if a liquid is an acid or a base. Indicators turn one color in acidic solutions and another color in basic solutions. If the liquid is neutral, the indicator color

Litmus paper, a type of indicator, turns red as it touches the acid of a lemon.

The acid of a bee sting can be neutralized with baking soda, a basic compound.

stays the same. For example, the water in a swimming pool should be neutral, neither acidic nor basic. By testing with an indicator, a person can determine if the water in a pool is safe.

Acid-base reactions have many practical uses. A good use of acid-base reactions is to stop the hurt of an insect sting. Wasp stings contain a basic compound, so dabbing a sting with a little vinegar, an acid, neutralizes the base. Bee stings are acidic, so one way to neutralize the pain is with baking soda.

Oxygen Reacts with Metal

Another family of reactions involves oxygen. Rusting and burning are reactions with oxygen. Some of these reactions occur very slowly while others happen at lightning speed.

Most cars, bridges, and nails contain iron. Oxygen in the air combines very easily with iron. When iron and oxygen combine, the reaction forms iron oxide, more commonly known as rust. The reaction of rusting takes a long time.

Once rust appears on a piece of metal, the rust will flake off. This exposes another layer of iron to oxygen, so more rust forms and flakes off. Eventually the entire piece of metal will disappear. It usually takes years for an old car or metal bar to rust to nothing.

For the reaction that forms rust to occur, the oxygen has to come into contact with the iron. Painting cars and bridges protects the metal from oxygen and keeps them from rusting.

A shipwrecked boat lies covered in iron oxide, more commonly known as rust (inset).

Other metals also combine with oxygen in this family of reactions. The Statue of Liberty is covered with copper metal. The copper reacted with oxygen and acid in the air, forming copper oxide. The green copper oxide does not flake off like iron oxide, so oxygen cannot reach the next level of copper. The copper oxide protects the rest of the copper on the statue.

Oxygen Feeds Fire

Some reactions with oxygen happen quickly. Burning is one. When a piece of wood burns, the materials in the wood combine with the oxygen in the air. The products of this reaction are carbon dioxide, carbon ash, and energy. A person can see the reaction taking place. In a few hours, a fire can burn several logs. It does not take years like rusting does.

When the chemical bonds of the wood break apart and form new bonds with the oxygen, energy is released. The energy is heat and light, so the fire warms and provides light.

Fires must have oxygen to keep burning, so firefighters use techniques to smother a fire to stop it. Water, sand, blankets, and foam keep oxygen away from the burning material and stop the fire.

An extremely fast reaction with oxygen happens with rocket engines. Rockets carry fuel and liquid oxygen. When ignited, the fuel and oxygen react quickly and produce gases that force the rocket up. This reaction releases a tremendous amount of energy to lift the rocket.

Rocket fuel and oxygen combine to produce gases that launch the space shuttle.

Electrical Reactions

One family of reactions involves electrons and electricity. Electricity is a stream of moving electrons, so these reactions can be used to make electricity. A battery produces electricity through a chemical reaction.

A flashlight battery has two terminals, one with a negative charge and one with a positive charge. The negative terminal is a zinc rod, a metal that loses electrons easily. Around the zinc is a mixture that is a base. The basic compound causes a chemical reaction in the zinc and each zinc atom loses two electrons. The electrons move toward the other terminal because they are attracted to the positive charge, in the same way that opposite poles of magnets attract each other. At the positive terminal, the electrons react with another compound. The movement of the electrons heats up a wire and makes a light bulb glow as the electrons pass through it. The battery is dead when the zinc rod is used up and no more electrons can flow.

Reactions that release electrons and produce electricity can be used to deposit metal on top of other metals. Fancy silverware is usually a cheaper metal underneath that has been covered with silver. The utensils are hooked up to electricity in a solution of silver salt molecules. The silver atoms in the solution are missing one electron, giving them a positive charge. When the electricity is on, the positively charged silver atoms are attracted to the metal utensil because it has a negative charge and extra electrons. Silver atoms stick to the metal by taking electrons from the cheaper metal. The coating of silver makes the metal look like solid silver. The process is much like painting a house.

Huge Molecules

Another family of chemical reactions results in huge molecules. The water molecule has three atoms, two hydrogens and one oxygen. But some molecules have hundreds of atoms that react with each other and form long chains. These huge molecules are called **polymers**, meaning many parts. Some polymers, such as hair, fur, and cotton exist in nature. But many are made in laboratories. The most common is plastic.

Different molecules can react to make all kinds of plastics. One type of molecule reacts into long chains and the final product is flexible plastic wrap. A different type of molecule can also form long polymer chains and the result is hard plastic like a comb. A third starting molecule produces a polymer used in baby diapers that can absorb up to one hundred times its weight of water. Each family of reactions has its own characteristics that can be used to predict how reactions between other chemicals will happen.

Chapter 3

Life Reactions

Important chemical reactions not only happen in beakers and factories. Critical reactions take place in plants and in our bodies. People could not survive without these reactions. Breathing, getting energy from food, and the healing power of medicine all depend on chemical reactions.

Plants React

Just like animals, plants need food to have energy to grow. Plants get food through **photosynthesis**. The word photosynthesis comes from two words: *photo*, meaning "light", and *synthesis*, meaning "to make something." Photosynthesis is a set of chemical reactions that combine carbon dioxide from the air, molecules from the plant, water, and sunlight to produce energy for the plant to grow.

During photosynthesis, plants take in water from the soil and carbon dioxide from the air. When sunlight hits a leaf, the leaf absorbs the sun's energy. It does this with the help of chlorophyll, a molecule found in

How Photosynthesis Works

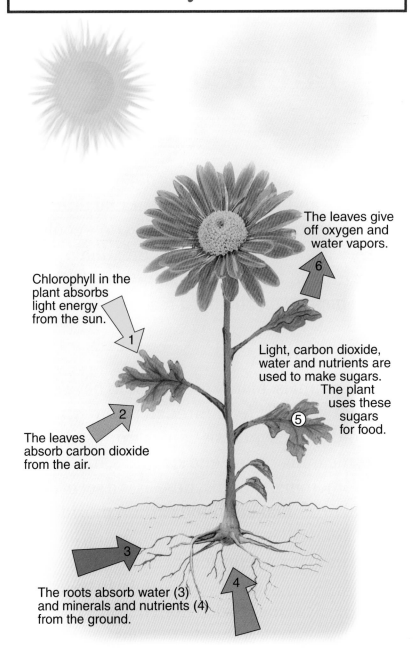

The leaves give off oxygen and water vapors.

Chlorophyll in the plant absorbs light energy from the sun.

Light, carbon dioxide, water and nutrients are used to make sugars. The plant uses these sugars for food.

The leaves absorb carbon dioxide from the air.

The roots absorb water (3) and minerals and nutrients (4) from the ground.

all green plants. Hydrogen atoms from water pick up the energy from the chlorophyll and use it to combine with carbon atoms from carbon dioxide in the air. This reaction makes sugar molecules that the plant uses to grow. In this way, the plant makes its own food.

A plant requires sunlight to grow. If a plant is left in darkness, the chlorophyll cannot get energy, so the reaction cannot happen. The leaves will fade and eventually the plant will die.

In photosynthesis, water and carbon dioxide use the energy of the sun to react and form the products of sugar and oxygen. The oxygen is released back into the air, so it is available to be breathed by animals and people.

Breathe In

People cannot survive without breathing, or **respiration** as it is also called. Respiration is a series of chemical reactions. Much like burning, respiration requires oxygen.

When people breathe in, they pull air into their lungs. The vital part of air is oxygen. Oxygen makes up about one-fifth of the volume of air. The rest of air is mostly nitrogen, which is not used in respiration. The oxygen in air is a molecule containing two atoms of oxygen bonded together.

When air reaches the sacs inside the lungs, the oxygen molecule squeezes through the cell wall and into the tiny blood vessels around the lungs. Here

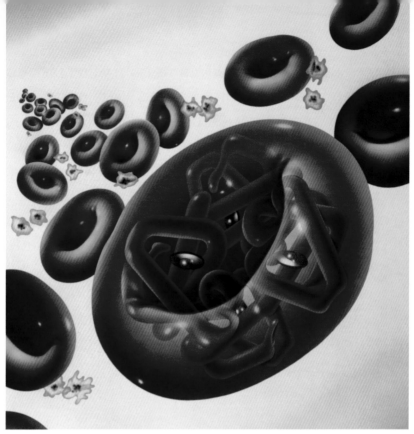

In this computer illustration of a blood cell, oxygen molecules (green) bond with hemoglobin molecules, giving the cell its red color.

the oxygen bonds with a huge molecule in blood. This molecule is known as hemoglobin.

The bonded hemoglobin-oxygen molecule gives blood its red color. As the heart pumps the blood, the hemoglobin-oxygen molecule sweeps past cells of the body. These cells need oxygen to do their work, so the oxygen atoms come loose from the hemoglobin and enter the cell.

Each cell needs energy to work. The cells use oxygen to produce heat, which keeps the body warm and provides energy for muscles to work.

Besides the heat used by the cells, the respiration reaction produces carbon dioxide. The cells unload the carbon dioxide into the blood and the hemoglobin carries it to the lungs. In the lungs the carbon dioxide squeezes through cell walls and is released when the person exhales.

Digestion Reactions

During respiration, the tiny oxygen molecules squeeze through the cell walls in the lungs. When a person eats, the molecules in the food are too big to squeeze into the cells of the body. So the food molecules must be smaller. Digestion is a series of chemical reactions that take food molecules apart and make them small enough to fit into the cells. About fifty chemicals break down food so the body can use it.

The first reaction starts in the mouth. As a person chews on a sandwich, for example, the food mixes with spit, or saliva. Chemicals in the saliva start breaking the bonds of the starch molecules in the food. Starch molecules come from foods such as breads and cereals.

Once the food is swallowed, acid and other chemicals in the stomach react with it and break the big molecules apart. Fat and protein molecules from meats and dairy products are cut up into smaller molecules.

In the small intestine, even more chemicals produced by the liver, pancreas, and gallbladder digest the food. By now, the large molecules that started

Digestion

Chemical reactions in the body break down food molecules for use by the body's cells.

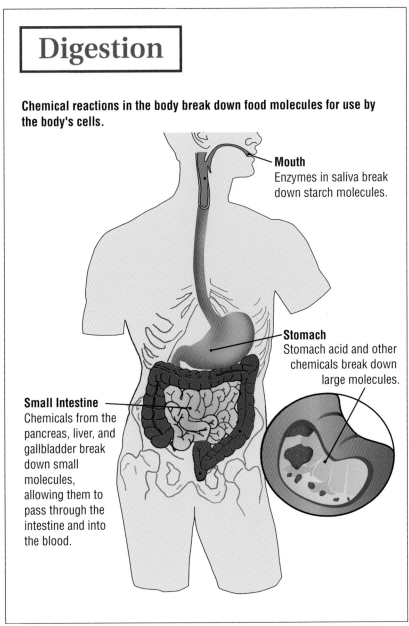

Mouth
Enzymes in saliva break down starch molecules.

Stomach
Stomach acid and other chemicals break down large molecules.

Small Intestine
Chemicals from the pancreas, liver, and gallbladder break down small molecules, allowing them to pass through the intestine and into the blood.

out in the food are broken into molecules small enough to pass through the walls of the intestine and into the blood. The blood carries the food to all the cells of the body to be used as energy for the work of each cell. The leftovers of the food that the body cannot use pass out of the large intestine.

Medicines Stop Reactions

When a person is sick, medicine is often taken to help heal the illness. Medicines work in many different ways, but most of them involve chemical reactions.

If a person has a bacterial infection, such as strep throat, antibiotics may be prescribed. Antibiotics, such as penicillin, prevent chemical reactions that allow bacteria to grow. Bacteria thrive by building strong cell walls. Chemical reactions allow bacteria to link molecules, like a net, to form a strong wall. The antibiotic prevents this reaction, so the cell wall stays weak. Eventually the bacteria cell ruptures and the body can clean up the infection.

Some antibiotics work by keeping bacteria from performing the chemical reactions required to reproduce and make other bacteria. The bacteria die and there are no new ones to make the person sick.

When a person has a headache or fever, they often take acetaminophen. Pain or fever is caused by chemical reactions in the cells of the body. Acetaminophen stops this reaction and the pain or fever goes away.

Asthma is a condition that sometimes makes it hard for a person to breathe. The muscles in the tubes

A girl suffering from asthma uses an inhaler to help her breathe.

of the lungs tighten up in an asthma attack. The tightening up makes it hard for the person to pull air into his or her lungs. Asthma medications stop the tightness by reacting with muscle cells and making them relax. Then the person can breathe easier.

A chemical reaction can even protect a cut. New products for sale are spray-on liquid bandages used to cover a cut or scratch. The spray contains a chemical that bonds with water molecules in the skin to make long polymer glue molecules. The reaction happens very quickly. The glue seals the edges of a wound so it can heal and be protected. After about a week, the bonds of the polymer break down naturally and the glue flakes off the skin. By that time, the wound has healed.

Plants perform chemical reactions to grow and provide food for us. Reactions also allow us to breathe, digest food, and heal our bodies.

Chapter 4

Exotic Reactions

Scientists want to increase their knowledge about chemical reactions. By understanding chemical reactions, they hope to decrease pollution and make more efficient cars and faster computers.

Ozone: Good and Bad

One reaction that scientists want to know more about is the chemical reaction that produces ozone. Ozone is a gas that contains three oxygen atoms bonded together. The oxygen that people breathe is a molecule with two oxygen atoms. Ozone can be good or bad for us, depending on where it is in the atmosphere.

Ozone in the air close to earth adds to air pollution. Breathing ozone is bad for people and animals, causing damage to lungs. Plants suffer, too. Too much ozone in the air causes weaker plants with smaller yields.

So how do we get ozone? Exhaust gases from cars, from fossil fuel power plants, and other pollutants react in the sunlight to form ozone. Ozone pollution is a concern in countries around the world. Many countries are trying to learn about the chemical reactions that produce ozone.

NASA, for example, has a program to track ozone and help develop ways to reduce the amount in the air. Using satellites and ground weather stations, scientists hope to learn more about how ozone forms and how to keep it from hurting people, animals, and plants.

Exhaust gases from fossil fuel power plants and cars combine with oxygen to form ozone.

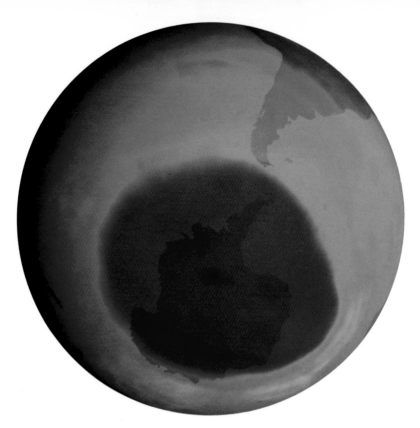

In this NASA image, the large hole in the ozone layer over Antarctica is shown in blue.

One strange thing about ozone is that we also need it to survive. But the ozone that is good for us is much higher in the atmosphere than the ozone that harms us. In the upper atmosphere, high above earth, ozone is produced by oxygen molecules reacting with single oxygen atoms. This reaction forms the three oxygen molecule. The part of the sunlight that causes sunburn and skin cancer is absorbed by ozone molecules. If more of this sunlight reached earth, people, animals, and plants would die. So in this case, ozone acts as our protector, a blanket that shields us from the harmful effects of the sun.

In recent years, scientists learned that the amount of ozone in the upper atmosphere was decreasing. Research showed that one cause was the reaction between ozone and some chemicals used in air conditioners and spray cans. Chemists developed new chemicals for these uses that do not react with ozone. The levels of ozone in the upper atmosphere seem to be slowly increasing.

Reactions in Space

Experiments aboard the International Space Station have advanced our understanding of reactions that also occur on earth. Astronauts have performed experiments in growing protein crystals. Proteins form by the reaction of smaller molecules into huge molecules. Many of the important chemicals in the human body are proteins. Increasing knowledge of proteins and how they combine into huge molecules may lead to new medicines to cure diseases. On earth, gravity pulls at a protein crystal as it forms so the crystals sometimes are lopsided. In the **microgravity** of space, crystals grow bigger and more perfect. Scientists hope to learn more about the structure of proteins from these lessons.

Astronauts on the space shuttle have also studied how fires burn. Flames on earth are influenced by gravity and form into a teardrop shape as the gases released from the burning rise. In the microgravity of space, fireballs are formed and they burn with very little fuel. Learning more about how the fires burn with small amounts of fuel may help scientists build cars that use less gas and pollute less.

Exotic Fuel

One of the new fuels being studied is hydrogen. In the future, a person may drive up to a service station and fill his or her car with hydrogen. This would be possible once scientists develop better fuel cells that burn hydrogen. Fuel cells that burn hydrogen have been used in spacecraft, but they produce a lot of heat and are expensive. Scientists are working to

A General Motors engineer test-drives the Hy-wire, a car powered by hydrogen fuel cells.

find reactants that cost less and work at lower temperatures.

It is already possible to buy a car that burns hydrogen part of the time. The reaction of oxygen and hydrogen in the fuel cell produces heat that is used to make electricity and power the car. When the cars burn hydrogen, the exhaust is only water. When hydrogen is not available, these cars also can burn gasoline. Some pollution is still produced when the car burns gasoline. Once hydrogen is available at all gas stations and the fuel cells are cheaper, more people will be driving cars that burn only hydrogen.

Molecular Computers

Since the invention of the computer, engineers have been attempting to make computers faster and more powerful. Someday computers may be even smaller and faster because of molecules and chemical reactions. Molecular computers could approach the speed and power of the human brain.

Many chemical reactions are used today to manufacture the computer chips in electronic devices. The basic component of chips is an element, silicon. The silicon is covered and reacted with different chemicals to form the wires and switches that allow it to work as a computer chip. The process is like using a stencil to color letters on a poster.

The main ingredients of a computer chip are on-off switches that build memory devices. In today's

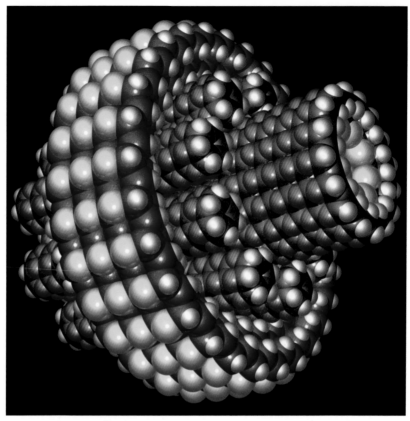

The molecular gear in this computer model might be used in the machines of the future.

computers, these are all built onto the silicon base. The size has gotten smaller and smaller. But chips made in today's fashion cannot get much smaller. Machines cannot make them any smaller without a cost of billions of dollars. The machines cannot make tinier lines in the stencil. A new manufacturing process must be found for faster computers.

In the future, the switches and memory devices may be only a few molecules. These switches would be about sixty thousand times smaller than the ones in today's computers. They also could be much cheaper to build.

Researchers are experimenting to learn how to build molecules that perform as computer components. One of the problems is how to link up the molecules. Another is how to get the molecules to stick in one place on the base material. Scientists continue to experiment with reactions and molecules to make them work as computer switches.

One advantage to molecular switches is that when molecules are made, they are all alike. Silicon switches and memory devices sometimes have flaws that keep them from working. But molecules of a chemical are identical. So using molecules in computer chips could do away with many flaws.

Scientists will continue to study chemical reactions both in space and on earth. As they learn more about how reactions occur, new products to help humankind will be developed and our knowledge of the world around us will grow.

Glossary

atoms: The smallest particles that combine and break apart in chemical reactions.

bond: The force that holds molecules together by sharing or exchanging electrons.

digestion: The process of breaking down food molecules so they can be used by the cells of the body.

electron: The particle that orbits the atomic nucleus.

microgravity: The small amount of gravity felt in space.

molecule: Atoms that react form bonds and combine into groups called molecules.

photosynthesis: The process that plants use to make their food by combining sunlight, water, and carbon dioxide.

polymer: A type of very large molecule such as plastic.

products: The results of a chemical reaction.

reactants: The chemicals that react in a chemical reaction.

respiration: The process of breathing and transporting oxygen to the cells of the body.

Books

Ann Fullick, *Chemicals in Action.* Des Plaines, IL: Heinemann Library, 2000. An interesting book that starts out explaining chemical reactions and continues with practical applications such as pollution, fossil fuels, and materials.

Don Nardo, *Atoms.* San Diego, CA: KidHaven, 2002. A well-written description of the building block of nature, the atom. Includes excellent examples showing the size of atoms and how they combine into molecules.

Ann Newmark, *Eyewitness Science: Chemistry.* New York: Dorling Kindersley, 1993. A comprehensive book about chemistry, including history of the science. Great illustrations and photographs enhance the text. A highly recommended reference book.

Steve Parker, *Look at Your Body: Digestion.* Brookfield, CT: Copper Beech Books, 1996. The explanations in this book are accompanied by impressive illustrations. It does an excellent job of explaining the process of digestion.

J.M. Pattern, *Acids and Bases*. Vero Beach, FL: Rourke, 1995. Good explanation of acids and bases and where they can be found. The book also covers the neutralization process and includes some experiments.

Bill Ross, *Straight from the Bear's Mouth: The Story of Photosynthesis*. New York: Atheneum Books for Young Readers, 1995. Through an amusing story about a bear, Ross relates the facts about photosynthesis. He leads the reader through experimental observations leading to conclusions about the best environment for plants.

Alvin Silverstein, Virginia Silverstein, and Robert Silverstein, *The Respiratory System*. New York: Twenty-first Century Books, 1994. This book has a thorough discussion of respiration, speech, and disease affecting our lungs.

Derek Walters, *Chemistry: Atoms, Molecules, and Elements*. New York: Franklin Watts, 1982. Chemical reactions of all different kinds are the mainstay of this book. Includes many practical applications that make it an important book for young readers.

Web Sites

ProTeacher Chemistry (www.proteacher.com/110052.shtml). A teacher's Web site containing several experiments that can be performed with materials found at home.

Rader's Chem4Kids (www.chem4kids.com). Chemistry section of the extensive science Web site maintained by Rader Kapili and created by Andrew Rader Studios.

Wonder Net: Your Science Place in Cyberspace (http://chemistry.org/portal/a/c/s/1/wondernetdisplay. html). Web site produced for elementary school-children by the American Chemical Society.

Index

Picture Credits

As a chemist by education, Roberta Baxter wants to inspire young readers to learn about and enjoy science. She has written articles about science and history for several magazines, as well as a teacher's guide on chemistry. She lives with her family in Colorado. This book is in honor of the author's father, Roy Lyndel Dawdy, her first chemistry teacher.